Nature's Cache

Also by Jayne Linke and published by Ginninderra Press

Moonbeams in the Bitter Rain

Jayne Linke
Nature's Cache

Acknowledgements

Some of these poems have been previously published:
'Kookaburra Chorus' in The Friends of the Waite Arboretum newsletter, No 52, Adelaide, 2007
'A Blue Flower Day' in *Positive Words*, 2007
'Waiting' in *Tamba*, 2007
'Muse Cruising', 'Esplanade', 'Prunus Tree' and 'Streamsong' in *Beyond the Rainbow*, No. 35, Mousetrap Media, Nimbin, 2008
'Esplanade' and 'Algae Calligraphy' in *Rewired*, Friendly Street Poets 32, 2008
'Sunflower Shiver' in *Studio*, 2008
'Kookaburra Chorus', 'Canine Eyes', 'Muse Cruising' and 'Esplanade' in *A Flower Between the Cracks*, Helen Sage, Affirm Press, South Melbourne, 2013
'Muse Cruising' and 'Kookaburra Chorus' in *Moonbeams in the Bitter Rain*, Ginninderra Press, 2017
'Gum Saplings' in *Wild*, Ginninderra Press, 2018

Nature's Cache
ISBN 978 1 76041 877 9
Copyright © text Jayne Linke 2020
Cover photo: sandid from Pixabay

First published 2020 by
GINNINDERRA PRESS
PO Box 3461 Port Adelaide 5015
www.ginninderrapress.com.au

To
Mother Earth
& all that lies therein.

And to
my sister Sarah, for kinship & courage & for the special
memories of a childhood shared.

Contents

Introduction	11

Part 1
Dry Creek Bed	15
Wetland Wallow	16
Wattle	17
The Old Wall	18
Muse Cruising	19
Nature's Cache	20
Pocket of Stillness	21
Sunflower Shiver	22
Monument of Truth	23
Kookaburra Chorus	24
Rock Face	25
Midnight Melee	26
Just Before Rain	27
Library Oaks	28
Jacaranda Jaunt	29
McElligott's Quarry	30
Hum	31
Holding Back Tide	32
Downpour	33
Hail	34
Carapace	35
Tree Tangle	36
Frogalogue	37
Canine Eyes	38
Alfresco Café Tree	39
Cliff	40
Gum Saplings	41

Cottage Ruin	42
Beach Formation	43
Jetty's Remedy	44
Anchor	45
Algae Calligraphy	46
Shell Starter	47
Esplanade	48
A Blue Flower Day	49

Part 2: Bright Fragments

Garden Gate	53
Pathway	53
Flowers	53
Waiting	54
Prunus Tree	54
Centrepiece	54
Ecstasy	55
Lacebark Tree	55
Flamboyance	55
Imago	56
Butterfly	56
Bellflowers	56
Magnolia Bud	57
Winsome Wisteria	57
Colour Opening	57
Summer Sun Hibiscus	58
Bamboo Bliss	58
Captured Run-off	58
Autumn	59
Pear Tree	59
Autumn Vineyard	59
Glory Vine	60

Warrigal Wavering	60
Bark Mosaic	60
River Red Rhapsody	61
Brownhill Creek Ballad	61
A Park Bench	61
Mid-morning Glitter	62
Kingfisher	62
Nest	62
Tadpoles	63
Frog-on-a-log	63
Blue Wren	63
Skink Scuttle	64
Birdsong	64
Gum Blossom	64
Mopoke	65
Dragonfly	65
Imagery	65
Winter Shower	66
Memorial Park	66
Waterfall	66
Stream Song	67
Bluebells	67
Thanks	68

Introduction

Many years ago, when travelling home from a university placement in the Adelaide Hills, Jayne sustained very severe injuries in a car accident. Yet despite the breadth and ongoing impact of her injuries, Jayne's snapshots of the natural world around her breathe with colour, vigour and life. Her chosen words are robust and motile – dreaming, frolicking, singing, growing, dancing, beckoning, enduring, persisting. Jayne's sunny nature, equanimity and linguistic playfulness remind us to savour each moment.

Long ago, when speaking about one's capacity to contribute, Martin Luther King Jr said, 'Anybody can serve. You don't have to have a college degree to serve. You need only a heart full of grace. A soul generated by love.'

Thank you, Jayne, for all that you are, for all that you evoke in others, for your lyrical gifts of grace.

Jayne's family
2020

Part 1

Dry Creek Bed

A sloping stairway is lined by creepers.
Yellow is sunlight and moss.

Trees line the banks; the creek bed dry.
From the treetops, a crow moans.

Wind sighs,
a quiet backdrop.

Wetland Wallow

The river surface is crinkly,
like felt or tissue paper.

A duck squalls,
like a twanging plank.

This pond is marked
by reeds, grasses and a jetty.

Wattle

Wild, wonderful, waving in the wind.

Among pines.

They bloom, echoing the sun's colour.

Trippers & hippies walk under their shade.

Lovers & others bask in their fragrance.

Elegantly they frame the hill's pathways.

The Old Wall

A stone wall, pitted with four holes;
it could line a Welsh country lane.

Beyond the holes is a wire for training
passionfruit or bougainvillea.

Sunlight is gathered here.
Sticks and bricks lie around,

like broken bones.

Muse Cruising

I run my fingers through the sand;
they're splayed out like a comb.

Here in this space I feel my way,
afraid to call it home,

but it can be my holiday;
a place to slide and roam

and play among the ripples
and wallow in a poem.

Nature's Cache

A crow and a wattlebird call,
piercing the morning lull.

The valley is striped
like a humbug lolly.

Shadows are cast by
gum trees and saplings.

Sunlight in this valley is dazzling,
like a jewel from a pirate's stash.

Pocket of Stillness

A lone duck surface-feeds;
water-bugs aplenty.

Dragonflies hover,
brown water reflects blue sky.

Here is a pocket of stillness,
not far from the city.

Sunflower Shiver

Like a lion, it's bold and bright.
Leaves have serrated edges.

Stem is strong,
flower's centre is dark.

Petals are long and tapering,
shivering in a bold shout of colour.

Monument of Truth

Flowering, towering –
lofty and grand,

a spectral stand
of monumental gums

mark the heart and arteries
of this pristine parkland.

Microcosmic canyon, inside the
imposing trunk, shelters nestlings;

a reduced fragment, I relate to their sighs,
fragility and vulnerability.

Can I tap from flowing sap
a similar shield?

A foreign concept,
it's beyond my call.

Kookaburra Chorus

Raucous,
rolling
xylophone.

You
so relieve
the city drone.

In silent wonder
I adore your chortle.

As you pick the sonic bones away,
the wonder of a brand-new day uncurls.

You ring the day in truly new!

Bring to our ears,
the glory
of
your
warring,
morning chorus.

Rock Face

It looks like Indian skin;
red-brown and earthy.

A crow flies overhead
in a sweeping line.

The wind soughs
like a breath exhaling.

Slow rain begins,
and a cocky shrieks.

Midnight Melee

Darkness closes clasping fingers;
the climbing frame of night.

I hear a night-time prelude;
a roof-drum roll as possums fight.

Haunting mopokes moon their song.
It soon becomes a singalong.

Goblins romp and fat trolls bask
behind the mask of darkness clasp.

By night-time's coven
spells are woven.

Magic's free,
just wait and see!

Just Before Rain

The
moment
before
rain
is

expectant;
waiting,
knowing –

like
a dream
of fulfilment.

Library Oaks

The trees could be a
living link, a seam.

Leaves reflect sunlight.
Bark is carob, mocha, sepia.

There's birdlife in the upper storey;
the trees a living corridor.

Underneath, folk share
conversations, speculations,

observations;
ideas hatched in the library.

Jacaranda Jaunt

Trunks &
branches;

dark &
gnarled,

in knots
along the footpath.

Three ahead; finished
with crêpe paper blooms.

Branches end in alphabet shapes.
Trunk could be a torso's silhouette.

Quietly,
a petal

falls.

McElligott's Quarry

It has a bare wall – sheer,
pimpled with young bushes.

The rocky wall is red-brown,
broken by slabs of shale & granite.

Yellow soursobs
colour it in.

Hum

At river's edge, a peeling gum sapling
like a sunburnt settler.

Beyond are reeds, a lake –
lovely to behold, along the walkway.

Insects hum, constant, reassuring;
a page in a volume.

Holding Back Tide

Sprawling fingers of green reach,
beseeching the sun's tender kiss.

Higher, insistent,
fiery patronage.

The solid strong wall is merely a 'hold';
a persistent fold in life's ironing.

Grim, set stones, fiercely resolute,
yet a stronghold for fertile new seed –

swollen, unfolding pressure of fresh bud.
'Life goes on.'

* Written about ivy climbing over an old wall

Downpour

Down it comes,
pelting the car roof.

Now and then, wind
blows the drops near horizontal.

It sounds like castanets,
looks like glitter or silken sparklers.

Tanks and dams fill up.
Gutters clog, then spill.

Trees look replete – content as
lined up patrons at the bar.

The sky delivers rain like bullets,
the onslaught helping our life cycle.

Hail

Clouds hang,
like a pack of wolves.

Trees whisper,
in hasty aggression.

The first drops
are big and slow.

Then sleet showers land in piles,
making a crunchy carpet.

Carapace

A bee's shell –
it's dead,

but the colour stays;
an echo, or shadow.

Wings as delicate
as lined gift-wrap.

Busy bee, now
static, inert, forlorn.

Tree Tangle

Broad at its base.
Subtle tones of grey and white.

Leaves hang down;
dangling khaki spearheads.

Pale bark, smooth
as a salamander.

Halfway up, dark branches
radiate like chapters.

Crows caw lazily
like dry old floorboards.

This is a tangle
to be relished.

Frogalogue

Frogs' soundtrack, timeless
like a xylophone.

Birds take the secondary music space.
A dark coot flips to the creek surface.

I smile – content,
taking in the frogalogue.

Canine Eyes

Molten eternal liquid;
submerging windows to your soul.

Deep, wise canine eyes – a bright surprise –
you seem asleep, then take a peep.

You coyly hide a vivid mind
behind closed lids.

I have to ask myself –
'What lies behind those distant eyes?'

A woven patch of mammal impulse,
upon which we just hypothesise.

Alfresco Café Tree

White bark rolls like
lace or crêpe paper.

This tree has tiny leaves;
wispy afterthoughts.

The foliage makes a
shadow on the footpath,

clear and see-through
as cellophane.

Cliff

Bitten rock face
indents the footpath.

Patterned with hollows,
immovable, frozen.

At its base, grow
grasses in shadow.

Gum Saplings

Like running paint
   or dripping teabags,
      their bark is brown on pale.
         They're like skewbald horses
            galloping along a grassy skyline.
           Tall and pencil-like;
              they're a knocked-over
                 box of Derwents.

Cottage Ruin

Red & grey frames of brick,
green mould on one chimney.

Purple wild flowers –
like a mottled bruise.

It stands on a hill; stark
& bold as a skeleton.

Beach Formation

The coast here is rippled
with dunes and wells.

Fronted by a rockery,
pierced by a jetty.

Seaweed lies in heaps,
darkly knotted.

Sandflies hover
and preen the seaweed.

Reed clumps and yellow daisies,
streak the rockery with bright colour.

A broad expanse of sky
makes a ceiling.

Jetty's Remedy

The jetty audience is kissed
from head to foot, sensually,

by angel's breath that is the wind.
A gift to skin, to nose, to ears

as sweaty ocean smells blow in
and Nature's pan pipes begin

their soothing jetty melody
which sends me off deliciously,

into a day-sleep
remedy.

Anchor

Subterranean stronghold,
hooked fast to earth.

The elements eat you out,
body blotted with billiard-ball barnacles.

Obscured jewel,
sedately waiting exposure.

Algae Calligraphy

There are clouds over the sea,
& drifts of seaweed.

Writing in the clouds,
like fingerprints on foggy windows

& in the drifts of seaweed,
calligraphy.

Shell Starter

A white shell lies
face up, in the sand.

It could have been left
there for inspiration.

Or it could be a pretty accident,
fallen from a child's bucket.

In the water it protected a shellfish;
maybe it adorned a reef.

I'll take it home.

In the sun, it will still have
a shadow, charcoal grey.

Esplanade

Edge of the sea
is peaceful,

like a
nesting animal

digging
earth.

A Blue Flower Day

Sky is a long reflection
in shallow space.

The sea
of our earth shines.

Moving breezes
shift violets and irises.

My own eyes have been
likened to corn flowers

by lovers
when lazily entwined.

Part 2

Bright Fragments

Garden Gate

A closed gate
is a book unopened.

Pathway

Pathway beckons me.
Drifts of sunlight intersect;
a comma on a page.

Flowers

Vivid, crouching among greenery,
they bathe in sunlight;
ornamental,
incidental.

Waiting

Dreaming in the arms
of this piece of paradise.
Stories wait in eyes.

Prunus Tree

Like a grey-limbed waif
it decorates the corner.
On the grass, it throws
a spangled shadow.

Centrepiece

Waterfall amid
chiselled gardens, white dripping
wisteria framed.

Ecstasy

Like a mandala,
a round, yellow sunflower –
a bee in the middle.

Lacebark Tree

Pink blooms underfoot.
Here, by the lacebark, I languish.
Calm stillness pervades.

Flamboyance

Tulips in tango – a couplet,
dancing as a pair.

Imago

Butterfly – all new like fresh paint;
vivid, psychedelic.
Wings – still
drying.

Butterfly

Stain glass fabric wings
now catch the wind –
it's off for
a ride.

Bellflowers

Visited by bees,
you can almost hear their peals!
Spread the joy of pollen.

Magnolia Bud

A work in progress, as yet unopened.
Beside it, a flower folded.

Winsome Wisteria

In the sunlight it tumbles in blue sprays,
curling & swelling
like the sea.

Colour Opening

Buds unfurling,
among them – an unshaven gardener,
armed with a spade.

Summer Sun Hibiscus

Orange blossoms,
amid green leaves;
emblems in themselves.

Bamboo Bliss

Curving, ballet-style,
regimented nature, growing
along the creek.

Captured Run-off

Shiny, but dark brown.
Pooled in a grove of saplings.
Water twinkles here.

Autumn

Leaves are turning red, orange, yellow;
sprouting from their twigs
like blowtorches.

Pear Tree

In autumn,
the Manchurian pear tree
is a sunset on a stick.

Autumn Vineyard

Like a yellow seahorse,
a single leaf curls
in a treble clef
shape.

Glory Vine

On the hills road a glory vine
grows in a glissando upon a shed –
leaves spreading, like beckoning hands.

Warrigal Wavering

Waxy, wheaten stalks
in the tentatively
shifting air.

Bark Mosaic

Sketchy & static –
a tumble of twigs & bark;
a gutter mosaic.

River Red Rhapsody

Split down the middle
but new leaves are green.
Strong, old; an enduring tree.

Brownhill Creek Ballad

Casual, sunlit by the creek,
grasses flicker in my eye span.
Blithely, a duck floats by.

A Park Bench

Wooden, painted pause –
it waits for weary people,
perching birdlife too.

Mid-morning Glitter

Catching sunshine, the lake core
throws glittering
light.

Kingfisher

Blue & gold, sharp beak.
Now, as it flies, colours explode.
Small kookaburra.

Nest

Finely woven & complex –
housing a clutch of eggs;
smooth drops of
possibilities.

Tadpoles

They're a black blob – a team,
not ready yet for growing legs.
Mozzies hum, the creek their habitat.

Frog-on-a-log

Hops on algae,
lands on lily,
in calm,
round
pond.

Blue Wren

Daintily poised on
a long grass stem.
Tiny racing heart,
long tail.

Skink Scuttle

A lone skink parades
then stage-freezes
with feet like
flowers.

Birdsong

Warbling, falling in
notes, clear and joyful;
the magpie's carol.

Gum Blossom

Tumbling from trees
in clusters, the gum blossom.
Bright crimson, so bold.

Mopoke

Muted, dark dream;
brown & grey changeling,
appears the mopoke.

Dragonfly

Elegant, landed
here on a lush, earthy stalk.
Bright blue, the thorax.

Imagery

Trees or the weather,
landscapes too – make up vistas;
the poet's workbench.

Winter Shower

Rain on the roof;
placating, persistent,
perpetual.

Memorial Park

Pale green light filters through leaves –
like a mosaic mirage, a shard
from a dream.

Waterfall

Like a flight
of birds'
wings.

Stream Song

Running water sings
a sweet song over gravel –
backing up the birds.

Bluebells

At the roadside here
they bob benignly, sunlit;
a country trance.

Thanks

Thank you to my family for their love and encouragement and for support given to my writing forays. Thank you to all those who maintain our parklands, gardens and bushland sanctuaries – their flora, fauna and natural vistas inspire. Examples include Woorabinda Bushland Reserves, Warrawong Sanctuary, Laratinga Wetlands, Urrbrae Wetlands, The Botanic Gardens at Adelaide, Mt Lofty and Wittunga, The Waite Arboretum, Carrick Hill and Brown Hill Creek Reserve. Thank you to the friendly staff at the Sheoak Café and Damien on Fisher – your smiles and double shot espressos energise. Thank you to Amelia Walker for her engaging workshops, lively prompts and wonderful validations. Thank you to Rebekah Popescu for her whimsical art sessions which fire dreams and imagination. Thank you to my mother Helen for our writing excursions, for safekeeping my poems, for compiling and submitting the manuscript. Thank you to my father Innes for our word games and for his humour and constancy.

Special thanks to Stephen and Brenda Matthews at Ginninderra Press whose contribution to poetry and to writers everywhere shines. Thank you for your belief and for the beautiful production of this anthology.

www.ingramcontent.com/pod-product-compliance
Lightning Source LLC
Chambersburg PA
CBHW062155100526
44589CB00014B/1851